My Child: Finding God in the Midst of Chaos

TIFFANY MCCULLOUGH

EDITED BY
NICOLE QUEEN

This book is dedicated to those who have struggled to understand our Heavenly Father's love. Christ's love lifts, transforms, and redeems. It's because of His love that we are eternally free.

Contents

Introduction

Have you ever desired to know the Father's love for you? Have you ever wondered, how and why a God who is so holy, pure, and just wants to love someone so wretched as man? Perhaps, there may have been a time when you questioned whether Abba Father would ever be able to love you after disobeying his Word. In such moments, you may have wondered if God the Father could ever forgive you, despite your deepest, darkest sins. Or, have you ever compared the shortcomings and imperfections of your earthly father's with that of an all-knowing, all-powerful Heavenly Father? If so, this book is for you.

Our Heavenly Father wants you to understand and know Him as your Father. Abba desires to draw you unto His love, so that you will never question or waver when it comes to Him being all you need. He has come to give you a personal encounter with the chambers of His love that neither death nor life can separate you from. The longing of our Heavenly Father has always been for His children to see and know Him as Father and Lord. The Word of God states, "When my father and my mother forsake me, then the Lord will take me up" (Psalm 27:10 KJV).

My child, hear the Word of the Lord for your life today. At no point does My heart cease to beat for you, nor does the breath I breathe cease to blow into your lungs. It is my desire to fill, refresh, restore, and revive you each day. My child, you are the apple of My eye, and no one can pluck you out of My hands. You belong to me, and I to you. Let heaven's floodgates open and build the waste places; allow me to make it fruitful. And as a result, you shall raise up the foundations of many generations because you have known My love.

My child, this is the appointed time I have set aside to personally give you My touch. I have written upon the pages of time, to catapult you in dimensions of My love, accelerating what many thought was dead. I, the Lord your God and Father, have made you alive! You will not die; you will live to declare the Word of the Lord! My child, there has never been a boundary or limitation that has ever subdued My kingdom. You are My child and I am your Father. Come closer to the arms of My love and learn from me.

— Abba Father

Abba Father

*For ye have not received the spirit of bondage again to
fear; but ye have received the Spirit of adoption,
whereby we cry, Abba, Father.*

— ROMANS 8:15

I am an heir of the Most High God!

Abba appears to sound cynical, apart from the term *father*,
because many have not identified themselves as actual sons and
daughters of God. Oftentimes, we hear the word father and
misappropriate it by contrasting the natural identifications of father to
our Heavenly Father. This can give off a distorted view of our adoption
into the spiritual Kingdom of our Heavenly Father.

Because of this, many find it difficult and challenging to embrace
such an authentic, all supreme, all-knowing, infinite God. Many times,
they stand on the outskirts of their Godly inheritance because they
cannot identify with Abba.

The connotation of father relates to the human instincts of familiarity. Depending on how a child relates to his or her father, this may give off a negative connection to Abba, our Heavenly Father.

The term Abba, an Aramaic word for father, was used by Jesus and Paul to address the relational side of God, stressing the importance of personal intimacy. Christ capitalized on the term *father*, as a way to help us identify our communion and fellowship as children of God. This relationship stresses the significance of kingdom fellowship— an abiding love that no evil force can penetrate. The love between Abba and all of mankind is distinct to us, as earth's touch has no relativity. Yet, His love can be found upon all creation and humankind.

⁓

Abba Father, thank You for allowing me to have relationship with You. In You, I experience the unconditional love of a Father. Despite my experiences with my earthly father, allow me to see you for who You are, and not define You based upon such.

Abba, You have been there since the beginning of time. Before I was ever thought of by man, You had me on Your mind.

Abba, my Father, You formed me in my mother's womb, making all things well. You declared that I am fearfully and wonderfully made; Your works are wonderful and I know that full well (Psalm 139:14).

Abba, You held me in the palm of Your Hands, cradling me every moment, ridding me of my fears. Your Word gave life when man spoke death.

Abba, You kissed me with the seal of Your Word, and anchored me in Your love. There's no greater love in all the earth that I have found like Yours.

Abba Father, teach me Your ways and let my foot not slip. Let Your path be established before me; help me to give careful thought to Your will. Let my feet be steadfast in all Your ways.

Abba Father, I ponder the moments we spend together. You are my rock, my solid place, and the one I can trust. When evil rises against me, You utilize Your authority and condemn it.

Abba Father, hold my hand and never let me go. I'm Your Child and You are my hiding place; You preserve me from trouble. You surround me with songs of deliverance.

Abba, I wait for Your Word. Feed me 'till I want no more. Let my cup run over as the wells of living water spring forth new life.

Thank You for being a good, loving Father. In Jesus' Name, Amen.

∽

Practical Steps:

- Grow to know *Abba* as Father.
- Receive *Abba Father's* love.
- Understand the distinction between your natural father and *Abba Father.*
- Adjust your spiritual view of *Abba Father.*

Father of Salvation

*I am the door: by me if any man enter in, he shall be
saved, and shall go in and out, and find pasture. The
thief cometh not, but for to steal, and to kill, and to
destroy: I am come that they might have life, and that
they might have it more abundantly. I am the good
shepherd: the good shepherd giveth his life for the
sheep.*

— JOHN 10:9-11

I am saved by the Blood of Jesus Christ!

Imagine yourself standing outside in the rain without an umbrella, hoping not to get wet. Our Father of Salvation not only sees your current situation, but desires to give you protection that far exceeds the rain. Imagine Him standing beside you, holding His umbrella, keeping you sheltered from the tumultuous rain storms of life. He longs to not only keep your physical body safe from the elements, but ensure the spiritual safety of your soul through His umbrella of salvation.

Salvation is the cord that connects us to our Heavenly Father. It gives us life in abundance and in its fullness. It is with this newness of life that we learn to take steps gradually, increasing in faith and maturity. When we dwell under the Father's umbrella of safety, we are protected from life's toils and snares.

The Father of Salvation anchors us through the cord of love, as we feed on the nutrients of His Word. As a baby that receives oxygen and nutrients through the umbilical cord, our faith in the Father of our salvation sustains us as we grow unto maturity.

Eventually, we will stretch out in faith and walk in empowerment and abundance. As the psalmist states, "On Christ the solid rock I stand. All other ground is sinking sand!" This pronouncement declares the security found in our Heavenly Father— the stability and solid foundation we can stand on, if Christ is applied to our lives.

Redemption cannot be found in anything or anyone other than the Father of Salvation. There is no other name under heaven given to mankind by which we must be saved (Acts 4:12).

⁓

Abba Father, You are the source of my salvation. You were right here all along. You have never left or forsaken me. You had my back all along.

When I look back over my life, I realize that there have been many times where I rejected You, turned my back on You, and idolized others before you. I've placed friendships, relationships, family, and success over you. However, I'm reminded in Your Word that I shall not worship any other god, except the Lord God Almighty, who is a jealous God.

Father, You alone are worthy of all my praise; You alone

deserve my worship. I lift up holy hands in adoration unto You, leaving all else and returning unto You.

The sacrifice of your death saved me from a life of sin, giving me an opportunity to live once again. Because of You, I have hope and eternal life in You. Thank You for saving me. Thank You for keeping me. I vow to live out the rest of my days in honor of Your grace, in full surrender to You! In Jesus' Name, Amen.

Practical Steps:

- Understand that Abba is the Savior of our soul and spirit.
- Accept salvation for eternal peace with Abba.
- Abide in Abba as He abides within you through the power of His salvation.

Father of Peace

And His name will be called Wonderful Counselor,
Mighty God, Eternal Father, Prince of Peace.

— ISAIAH 9:6B KJV

I am filled with God's peace that surpasses all understanding!

Have you ever noticed the relationship between a child and his or her earthly father? More times than not, if a healthy bond has been established, the child is more inclined to have open communication with the father or seek him for support when challenges arise. When this happens, it displays a level of comfort and peace within this special father and child relationship. This is what God desires for us, as our Heavenly Father.

Despite how impactful the relationship between a father and child may be, it doesn't compare to God's peace. The Bible reveals to us that God's peace surpasses all understanding and will keep our hearts and minds in Christ Jesus (Philippians 4:7). Therefore, it's important to understand that although our earthly parents may give us guidance, the source of our peace rests in God.

All of God's children have access to His peace. God alone, is the source of our peace. For us to experience peace with God, we must know who we are in Him, and understand where we are in our faith. Faith is essential to pleasing God. The key to experiencing peace with Him is believing in Jesus Christ and receiving all of what He has promised us through His sacrifice.

Once we establish peace with our Father, in turn, we will experience peace within ourselves. It's important to note that God does not promise freedom from conflict or challenges. However, He promises that we will overcome through our faith in Him, by resting in His peace for refreshment and renewal during trying circumstances.

Personal peace is received through our faith in Him. With His vast love and wisdom, trusting God to always provide for our needs is the key to personal peace. It becomes easier to receive what's rightfully ours — as Children of the Father of Peace— when we abstain from destructive thoughts and habits, and instead, focus on the truth of who God is. We must replace anxiety with confidence, disappointment with rejoicing, and confusion with assuredness.

~

Abba Father, I long for Your peace so that I can break free of negative thinking. I invite You into my mind so that you can begin transforming my thought patterns from the root. Please help me recognize, reject, and replace thoughts that are not pleasing to You.

Many times, it feels like I am clinging to the hinges of hope, as the whirlwinds of life fight to take hold of me. In such moments, it feels like I'm holding on to life by subtle gasps of breath, as my airways plunge to give its last fight for life.

Father of Peace, I exchange my mental chaos for Your

soundness of mind; You hold me in place when the cares of this world beat against my house made of flesh. I am held together as a result of my intimacy in You. You are the source of my nutrients, which come from the Word of God.

It is because of my faith in You, Father of Peace, that I've learned to hold on when life tells me to let go. The source of my peace is directly tied to the level of intimacy I have in You. Help me to grow closer in my fellowship with You. In Jesus' Name, Amen.

~

Practical Steps:

- Accept Abba's peace by knowing your position.
- Know Abba as a *peace* giver.
- Wear Abba's peace as a covering from the storms and cares of life.
- Walk in the peace of Abba, continuously.

Father of Promise

God is not a man, that He should lie; neither the Son of Man, that He should repent: hath He said, and shall He not do it? Or hath He spoken, and shall He not make it good?

— NUMBERS 23:19 KJV

I am a recipient of God's divine promises!

Have you or anyone you've ever known been let down because someone broke a promise they made to you? As some would say, that person didn't honor the word that was given. Oftentimes, what happens is, once a person has broken a promise that is important to you, you may find it difficult to put your trust in that individual. Therefore you may start to view that individual as someone who does not keep his or her word.

Being a promise keeper is very important when dealing with others. This attribute of God is something we can rest on. Our Heavenly Father keeps every promise He makes (Proverbs 30:5). We never have to worry about Him breaking a promise. He stands by His Word to make sure it's performed.

When we are faced with situations that seem to be frustrating, challenging, or vexing, we can go to God's Word of Promise and find scriptures that best fit our need and apply it like ointment, until it soothes every place. God's promises bring comfort as we trust His Word.

In the Word of God, we are assured of many promises. In Hebrews 13:5b, God has promised to never leave or abandon us in our time of need. Therefore, we can trust that He is always near, even if it's hard to feel His presence. He promised us that all things would work together for the good of those who love Him. And that's because He can see the end from the beginning and work everything out for our well-being.

He also promised us rest. In Matthew 11:28-30, He outlines the methodology for us to receive rest. When we are overwhelmed with the burden of responsibilities and intense schedules, we can give our stress over to Him and receive His rest. Living each day in His presence ensures that our priorities become His priorities and that we flow in accordance to His will.

Abba Father has also promised to lead and guide us. In John 14:26, we learn that He will help, teach, and bring things to our remembrance, according to His truth. This will enable us to steady the path of purpose.

～

Abba Father, thank You for always keeping Your promises. In Your Word, many promises can be discovered throughout. You are the God of salvation, hope, redemption, and life. The Word of God makes it clear that You desire all to be saved and redeemed back to You. Therefore, I can cling to Your promises, knowing that I can trust You with my soul.

Abba Father, You are a God of true restoration. You can take the broken pieces of my life and rebuild me into someone new. Apart from You, I cannot attain true healing, deliverance, or rest. I am most grateful for Your promise to transform my life from the root, enabling me to rest in the victory of Your peace.

But most importantly, Abba Father, thank You for the blessed gift of Your Son Jesus Christ, who has ensured me the beautiful promise of eternal life. The rest of my life is no longer in question. I have a solidified hope of eternal life in You. Thank You for this beautiful promise. In Jesus' Name, Amen.

Practical Steps:

- Identify the promises Abba has spoken over you.
- Receive Abba's promises in your life.
- Celebrate the fulfillment of Abba's promises.

Father of Guidance

*And the Lord shall guide thee continually, and satisfy thy
soul in drought, and make fat thy bones: and thou
shalt be like a watered garden, and like a spring of
water, whose waters fail not.*

— ISAIAH 58:11 KJV

I am safe under the direction of God!

When our footsteps are guided, we are led to the Rock who is higher than us. In such moments, we can take hold of God's Hand, knowing that His guidance will lead us to the right place. We may search the world or look to friends, family and organizations for direction— but to no avail. God is our ultimate source of guidance, as He knows our final destination.

Many times, when taking a road trip, we may take out a map or use GPS to get us to our destination. However, despite our best attempts for precise direction, we must understand that man-made devices and/or attempts have the propensity to fail. In moments like these God has proven the frailty of man's best attempts apart from him. It's when we're in Christ that we discover the pure guidance and genuine love of our Father's concern to get us to the right destination for our lives.

Many times we may want what we want and will sometimes fight God on what we think is best for our lives, not realizing our own efforts apart from Him only lead us to repetitive cycles and breakdowns in life. Then, we may find ourselves blaming God for trying to operate apart from His guidance. Our Heavenly Father gives us divine instructions for strategic moves. Each move we make in life guides us closer to our destination and fulfilled purpose.

When we think about a toddler, as they're learning to navigate through the phases of development, there are moments where the child may pull away from the caregiver to seek his or her own way. It's in those times that the toddler may have no clue of impending danger that may be harmful. For the most part, toddlers tend to focus on their independence apart from their caregivers to succeed at what they desire to accomplish. In John 15:5, Jesus tells us that apart from Him we can do nothing.

Our road map to a fulfilled life rests in God's Word; it's His parental instructions to attaining a fulfilled life before leaving earth. Our Heavenly Father's desire is that we flourish in all He has created us to be, as we embrace His guidance for our lives.

~

Abba Father, thank You for blessing me with the provision of guidance. I understand that You are the Source of all direction and wisdom.

Forgive me for getting ahead of Your plans and for taking matters into my own hands. Help me learn when to stop and consult You for direction. Your guidance is infallible; I never have to worry about making a wrong turn when I follow Your leading.

Help me, Abba Father, to embrace the divine leading of Your Holy Spirit. Your Spirit enables me to move boldly and assuredly along the path of Your will. Help me to crave Your presence more than anything else in life so that I can move in harmony with Your will.

I understand that sin and disobedience grieve Your Spirit and can diminish my ability to hear You clearly. Sin distorts my perspective and leads me along the path of death. So, help me, Abba Father, to repent and be free from the thoughts, behaviors, and actions that are displeasing to You.

The closer I am to You, the closer I am to my destination. Help me to never forget that. I love and honor You for being such a great God of grace! Thank You for forgiving me when I chose to obey the voices of others and made bad turns in life. Your grace has saved me from a path of destruction. I thank You for Your gracious gift of mercy and realigning me along my path. In Jesus Name, Amen.

Practical Steps:

- Allow Abba to direct your path.
- Receive Abba's love, as He guides us away from the pitfalls, snares, and traps of the enemy
- Honor Abba as the source for guidance.

Father of Provision

But seek ye first the kingdom of God, and his right-
eousness; and all these things shall be added unto you.

— MATTHEW 6:33 KJV

I am content because I have everything I need in Him!

J ust for a few moments, sit back and reflect. How much do you believe you're worth to our Heavenly Father? Do you see yourself the way that He sees you? What thoughts do you have about yourself?

The Word God states, "Behold the fowls of the air; for they sow not, neither do they reap, nor gather into barns, yet your heavenly father provides for them. Are you not worth more than many sparrows" (Matthew 6:26)? Therefore, we should never second guess our value or worth to Abba Father. He loves us far more than we can ever imagine. If only we could adopt the mindset of Abba Father and allow His truth enter into our mind. Our lives should reflect the truth of His Word and what He says about who we are to Him.

Matthew 7:11 states, "If ye then, being evil, know how to give good gifts unto your children, how much more shall your Heavenly Father which is in Heaven give good gifts to those who ask Him?" It is our Father's desire to lavish all that He is and has on His children. However, our utter resistance leads to discontentment, shame, doubt, and fear. Our disobedience makes us vulnerable to the attacks of the enemy when we fail to heed our Father's guidance and instruction towards a fulfilled life.

Trusting in Abba Father's provision aligns us with purpose fulfillment. When we shrink back out of fear, we limit Him from fully utilizing us in the way He desires. He has an amazing plan for our lives. Therefore, fear cannot be given power to abort the plan God has in store for our lives.

There is absolutely no situation that can usurp the provision or power of God. Absolutely nothing can catch Him by surprise. He is the Omnipotent One that maintains all power, knowledge, and authority! There is no need for us to fear any aspect of life when Abba Father is given full control over our lives. When we are humbly submitted to Him, we are positioned to receive all that He has in store for us!

~

Abba Father, thank You for Your beautiful gift of salvation. By receiving Your redemption, I am properly positioned to enjoy the benefits of your provision.

Being in You affords me the opportunity to have access to the many benefits that accompany Your presence. I count it as pure joy to know that there is no circumstance or situation that can limit Your ability to demonstrate full control. You are Jehovah-Jireh, the One who provides. Everything is Yours and You hold it all in Your Hands.

Abba Father, thank You for knowing every single one of

my needs. Thank You for always knowing every single detail and having a plan.

Forgive, me Abba Father, for refusing to trust You. Forgive me for doubting You, worrying, and trying to do things on my own, apart from Your wisdom. Help me to always remember that You are more than capable of accomplishing more than I could ever do on my own! Therefore, I humbly submit my selfish ways and desires to You. I submit my heart to You, as I repent from trying to manage my life on my own.

Abba Father, help me to remember that my life is not mine; my life is Yours. In everything that I do, help me to remember this vital truth. In Jesus Name, Amen.

Practical Steps:

- Recognize that Abba is the Source of all provision.
- Call upon Abba for any type of provision need.
- Accept that you are worthy to receive Abba's physical, spiritual, emotional, mental, and financial provision.
- Understand that Abba has an unending supply of provision.

Father of Healing

*Heal me, O Lord, and I shall be healed; save me, and I
shall be saved: for thou art my praise.*

— JEREMIAH 17:14

I am healed by the Blood of Jesus!

She braced herself, not knowing what His response would be. She was tired, lonely, exhausted, ashamed, and ready to relinquish her search. For many years, she suffered with an issue that only Jesus could heal. She searched out many physicians— possibly even sorcerers— but to no avail, as her issue was still there. This woman, as denoted in Matthew 9:20-22, is referred to as "the woman with the issue of blood."

Although female, this woman represents both males and females alike who have suffered with widespread issues such as: anger, disease, disability, hurt, mental disorders, sexual disorders, drinking disorders, eating disorders, abuse, timidity, and low self-esteem, upon many others.

But don't lose hope! Abba Father is coming your way to see about you. You are His Child.

Our Heavenly Father has taken the time to personally come see about you. Every hurt you feel, pain you bear, and disappointment you experience, the Father says: *Give it to me, My Child.* There is no pain, weight, or burden too heavy for the Father, despite it being too heavy for us to carry.

In this moment, the Father is saying to you:

Come to me, you who are weary and burdened, and I will give you rest. My Child, take My yoke upon you and learn from Me, for I am gentle and humble in heart and you will find rest for your souls. For My yoke is easy and My burden is light. I am He who forgives all your sin and heals all your diseases.

— PSALM 103:3

Throughout my entire life, the best healer I have ever known is our Heavenly Father. He not only provides a remedy, but He secures the antidote to ensure that we are restored back to wholeness. This is not to say sickness, disease, or natural things won't come— as they may. However, He promises to heal us from them all.

Our Father understands that in a fallen world, we won't always make the best decisions or always approach life the correct way. So, this is where we embrace the gift of Jesus Christ by receiving Him as Lord of our lives. This ultimately helps us avoid some of the pitfalls we willingly and/or unknowingly walk into.

Through Christ's divine healing and instruction, we can live a life of wholeness. To experience this change, we must accept Abba Father's spiritual, mental, and physical healing for our lives. It simply requires a posture of surrender and a choice to receive.

Oftentimes, we don't always recognize Christ as the Source— *first.* As a result, we may find ourselves looking to people, material things, physicians, and other sources for our healing. However, we must respond like the woman with the issue of blood. Although she was tired and drained, she immediately recognized hope as soon as Jesus came on the scene! As she began to press her tired, worn body through the crowd, barely making it as the crowd bombarded her, she pushed and pushed until her press caused her to reach Jesus. The woman said to herself, "If I can just touch the hem of his garment, I will be made whole." And because of her faith, she was made whole!

This woman's faith caused her to push. Even when her body couldn't feel its impending healing, her faith caused her to push, despite what her senses were telling her! Therefore, she grabbed ahold of Jesus' garment and received her healing. In that instant, Jesus experienced virtue leaving His body, as a result of her faith.

Our Heavenly Father came so that you might have life in abundance, and within that inheritance is your healing. Embrace the Father's touch.

~

Abba Father, thank You for blessing me with Your Hand of healing. Help me to understand that healing is what You desire for me to receive, as You don't want Your children to suffer lack or dysfunction.

Abba Father, I thank You for always having my best interest at heart. You said in Your Word that healing is the children's bread. It's by Your heart of compassion that You are moved to heal the sick, raise the dead, and cast out demons! You desire good health for Your people.

Abba Father, You make it clear in 1 Peter 2:24 that Jesus Christ bore the weight of our sin in His body so that I might live in righteousness and be healed. It's because of Christ's atonement that I now have life! Because He was wounded and bruised for my transgressions, I can now experience true healing in every area of my life.

*As Your Child, help me to understand that Your sacrifice bought my healing! I no longer have to worry or wonder if You "can" heal or "will" heal, as Your Word has already assured me that I **am** healed! So, I thank You for this tremendous gift of Your love. In Jesus' Name, Amen.*

~

Practical Steps:

- Allow Abba to heal your soul, mend your broken heart, and restore your identity as His Child.
- Receive in your soul that there is nothing Abba cannot do.
- Believe that Abba will heal your family.

Father of Deliverance

The righteous cry, and the Lord heareth, and delivereth them out of all their troubles.

— PSALM 34:17

I am safe because the Lord delivered me!

When your faith is being tried by fire, what do you do? In most instances, some would pray to Abba Father or do something else they deem fit. Some may even sing or shout. However, there are times in each of our lives when we are faced with a bitter pain that leaves us numb to prayer, singing, and shouting. Sometimes pain, test, chaos, trials, and/or turmoil have a way of showing up at our doorsteps uninvited and unannounced. And sometimes, we may have to ask ourselves: *Where did this come from? How did this come about? Did I do something wrong? God, why me?*

Many of these unanswered questions may float over our heads. While we're attempting to work through our faith, it may feel like it's being tested by fire. Therefore, let's consider the story of three young men of great faith.

The faith of Shadrach, Meshach, and Abindigo was put to the test. They were admonished to worship a foreign god, but refused to bow down to the king's image. As a result of their disobedience to the king, they were thrown into a fiery furnace that was turned up ten times hotter. However, they were not destroyed and their clothes did not smell like smoke. Jesus was right there in the midst of the fire with them.

When considering this scenario, it's hard not to see that this is truly the rhetoric of our lives. When we look back over our lives, I'm certain that there have been many things we can recall that have tried our faith. In such times, we may have felt as if we weren't going to make it, and therefore, wanted to give up.

Life, however, has a way of showing up and showing out. But we must remember that in our furnace of affliction, Abba Father is right there with us, even when we can't trace Him.

In this moment, the Father is saying to you:

Fear not; for I am with you: be not dismayed; for I am your Father: I will strengthen you; yea, I will help you; yea, I will uphold you with my right hand of my righteousness.

— ISAIAH 41:10

Knowing this, the trying of your faith worketh patience. But let patience have her perfect work, that you may be perfect and entire, wanting nothing.

— JAMES 1:4

Deliverance annotates a synoptic of a personal encounter and experience of supernatural deliverance. In one's personal encounter with salvation, a supernatural impartation of regeneration has taken place. Transition has taken place. Heaven has shifted man's moral character from the love and life of sin, to the love of God and a life of righteousness. This is a sealing of rebirth, which many may refer to as being *born again,* as we are now born of the spirit, and not just the flesh.

A new birth is a heavenly birth that causes one to be made alive, spiritually. Where there was death, trespasses, and sin, Abba Father has now established new life due to being regenerated by His spirit. And now, one can see a new creation in Christ Jesus. So, this supernatural deliverance is by far the greatest encounter any man could ever experience along the lines of deliverance.

Our life means everything to the Father. It is His desire that none perish for lack of knowledge. Abba Father has given us treasures in heaven where neither moth nor rust doth corrupt, and where thieves do not break through to steal. Therefore, our deliverance already took place decades ago on the Cross. We are now obligated to walk in it! It belongs to us.

> *Abba Father, thank You for delivering me from the grip of sin. In You, there is abundant life for my soul! I no longer have to be in bondage to the effects of sin because of the immaculate grace of Jesus Christ!*

> *Abba Father, thank You for rescuing me from myself. You are the breaker of negative thoughts, distorted mind-sets, and shame. Your helmet of salvation covers my mind and is a reminder of who I am in You. I am Your Child.*

> *Your Word assures me in Psalm 32:7 that You are my hiding place and that You will protect me from trouble and surround me with songs of deliverance! So, I thank You for being my deliverer in times of overwhelm and confusion. Your truth is always there to keep me safe! I am thankful that You hear my cry and deliver me from all of my trouble (Psalm 34:17).*

I acknowledge Your sovereignty and humble myself before Your throne of grace. I receive Your love, grace, and protection. In Jesus' Name, Amen.

~

Practical Steps:

- Allow Abba to fully deliver you because prolonged avoidance does not equate to healing.
- Understand that there is delivery in deliverance.
- Accept that you are free from limitation in Abba.
- Find yourself Abba to experience the point of no return.

Father of Power

*Thine, O Lord is the greatness, and the power, and the
glory, and the victory, and the majesty: for all that is
in the heaven and in the earth is thine; thine is the
kingdom, O Lord, and thou art exalted as head
above all.*

— 1 CHRONICLES 29:11

I am anointed with the power of Jesus Christ!

A s a child, we often see our daddy as one who is strong and powerful— kind of like Superman, Batman, or the Green Goblin. But whichever you choose, his strength was identified by way of your favorite character. Somehow, as the reality of life hits, you're faced with obstacles that no one can save you from— not even your dad, your superhero. Suddenly, you may come to grips, realizing that this was God's intention; only He can fix that challenge in your life!

The Father of Power lends His Hand to the one that comes to Him as a child, who doesn't fear the vulnerability that comes with entrusting Him with our weakness. However, when we understand our weakness and accept His power as supreme, then, we are made strong!

Abba Father desires to hold you up when you can't keep yourself afloat. He desires to be your strength, yet without enabling you to stand on your own. It is your faith in the Father's words that teaches you to rest on His guidance and instruction. Therefore, you will be able to stand on your own, as you stand upon Him— the Rock.

The Father of Power gives us a clear view of a child who runs to his or her father in a moment of frailty, after taking a fall upon the ground, after scraping his or her bare skin. As a result, the child may be left with scrapes and bruises that need healing. And in painful agony, the child may look to daddy or mommy to provide care and to comfort him or her with love after experiencing a painful situation. To the child, it may appear to be a drastic situation. But to the parent, it may only be a minor cut with barely any blood. And because of the love and comfort from the parent, the child may fail to remember the degree of pain that was once experienced.

In comparison, our Father of Power manifests love above human capacity and normality, giving His children both natural and spiritual healing for complete wholeness and durability. The Father of Power gives us strength beyond human comprehension. It is in the midst of chaos, calamity, and challenges, that we begin to define our inherited strength. The Father of all fathers has given us His Spirit so that we may find Him in moments of weakness and frailty.

～

Abba Father, thank You for being so powerful in my life. I am grateful that You are a God who can take care of all of my needs, regardless of how intense they may be. Your power is unmatched. Nothing can compare to the power You possess.

Abba Father, I honor You for Your life-changing power in my life. It took the power of Your spirit to heal my brokenness and save me from the damnation of sin. Your incredible power has kept me safe from the effects of sin. Despite the bad decisions I've made in my life, your powerful love has continued to keep me throughout it all.

Thank You, Abba Father, for being my hero. Sometimes I may forget the true nature of who You are because it's easy to become so infatuated by everything that's going on around me. However, help me to always remember that You are the ultimate source of power and strength. It's in You that I can find true freedom, liberty, and life. Because of Your power, I have everything I need. In Jesus' Name, Amen.

~

Practical Steps:

- Understand that Abba is all-powerful.
- Accept Abba in your life as your Hero.
- Recognize that through Abba, we find strength.

Father of Victory

Ye are of God, little children, and have overcome them:
because greater is he that is in you, than he that is in
the world.

— 1 JOHN 4:4

I am victorious because God is within me!

They were racing toward the finish line, panting as their relinquishing gasp filled the air.

As the crowds cheered the participants on towards the finish line, there was one woman who stood out, as she swiftly passed her opponents. In her mind, she somehow believed that it'd be impossible to pass her opponents and achieve victory. However, as she continued around the track— in view— she saw the ribbon and the crowds standing on the sidelines. So she pressed in more, moving up to third place, then second.

Despite having achieved progress, her opponent seemed to be leading the way of what seemed to be a lifelong journey of great expectation. However, within herself, she knew that she could not give up. So she said to herself, *here goes*! And in that moment, she took another breath of air, pressed in harder, and gave it all that she had! She pressed in towards the finish line and the gun was fired! She won the race! The race was over, as this woman won the victory!

So, you may be wondering, *what's the significance of this story?* Many times, our lives can feel just like that. We may experience fluctuating emotions, a racing heart, rising tensions, or an excitement of mixed emotions, while running our life's race. Therefore, since we are surrounded by such a great cloud of witnesses, let us throw off everything that hinders or entangles us— to include, doubt, hatred, bitterness, unforgiveness, animosity, jealousy, pride, lust, perversions, lying spirits, gluttony, and fear, amongst many others.

So, let us run the race marked out for us with perseverance! Our victory is through the precious Blood of Jesus Christ! Our DNA has already sealed our victory! As a result, each of His Children can enjoy the benefits of His sustained victory! So, despite the many things that may try to entangle us, we must keep our eyes fixed on Jesus, Who is the prize of our finished race!

⌇

Abba Father, thank You for the victory we have in You. Because of the shed Blood of Your Son Jesus Christ, death was conquered and no longer has a sting! As Your Children, we now have victory through Jesus Christ. This victory is a constant benefit for all of Your Children.

Abba Father, I know that life has its share of ups and downs. But no matter what may be happening around me, my victory in You can never be compromised. I am so blessed to be Your Child and to have everlasting life in You.

Help me, Abba Father, to understand that no matter

what fear tactic the enemy uses, it can never usurp the power and dominion that Your victory maintains. You are a Father who loves Your Children.

Your victory is what has given me life and freedom! I am no longer in bondage to any pain of the past, confusion about the present, or fear of the future. There is nothing but freedom and peace because Your victory has given me security in my future.

Abba Father, I thank You for your relentless love for me. I thank You that I have nothing to fear— not now, not ever! In Jesus' mighty Name, Amen.

∾

Practical Steps:

- Abba gives us full access to His victory.
- Accept that because of Abba, the enemy of fear, doubt, abandonment, rejection, self-sabotage, low self-esteem, poverty, sickness, divorce, rejection, obesity, etc. has already been defeated.
- Wave your flag and proclaim your victory in Abba.

Father of Presence

*And he said, My presence shall go with thee, and I will
give thee rest.*

— EXODUS 33:14

I am fulfilled because I live in the presence of God!

My Child, do not let the words of others negatively influence
you or allow you to feel that for one moment that I don't
care. I know there are times you may question My presence, wondering whether or not I'm there with you. I've come to reassure you that I am near.

My Child, be still and know that I am the Lord, God, and Father of all. I love each of My children. However, for some, their hearts have turned away from me. Therefore, I'm calling for all of you who are lost to come home and abide in My presence.

My Child, allow My words to dance with you, creating a tapestry of beautiful artwork upon your heart. No eye has seen, no ear has heard, and no human mind has conceived the things that I, Your Father, has prepared for those who love me.

My Child, it's My desire to usher you into My holy presence, occupying your heart with nothing but Me. It's my desire to give you the good of the land, for evildoers will perish, but those that belong in My fold shall live. I am Abba, your Father, Creator of all mankind. My presence shall go with you and I will give you rest.

My Child, in Me you will find boldness and confidence. I will make known to you the path of life. In My presence, there is fullness of joy; in my right hand there are pleasures, forevermore.

~

Abba Father, thank You for Your sweet presence in my life. Because of You, I have access to everything I need. Everywhere You are present, there is fullness of peace and joy. It's impossible to live life without You. I thrive off of the purity of Your presence.

Just as a child who may be running around aimlessly, preoccupied with other activities, my heart immediately leaps at the entrance of Your presence. I can never take for granted the impact of Your divine presence in my life. Wherever You go, I want to be present. I need to be where You are!

Abba Father, I cannot survive life apart from Your presence. Help me understand that when challenges come, my first response should be to look up and give the situation to You. I should never respond in fear, worry, or anxiety. My response should always be one of faith, with the confidence that You are always with me! In Jesus' Name, Amen.

~

Practical Steps:

- Understand that Abba is an all-consuming presence.
- Recognize that Abba's presence can consume you naturally, in comparison to spiritually.
- Accept that Abba is everywhere we go.
- Grant Abba free access into your life.

Father of Righteousness

For he hath made him to be sin for us, who knew no sin;
that we might be made the righteousness of God
in him.

— 2 CORINTHIANS 5:21

I am justified because of His righteousness!

My Child, because you have believed in Me when everything else around you failed, it has been credited unto you as righteousness. For in righteousness, I am revealed from faith to faith.

As it is written, the righteous man shall live by faith. For this reason, it is by faith, so that it may be in accordance with grace. This is so that the promise will be guaranteed to all My descendants— not only to those who are of the law, but also to those who are of the faith of Abraham, who is the father of us all.

For all have sinned and fall short of the glory of God. Therefore, receive justification as a gift by My grace through redemption, which is in My Son, Christ Jesus. Understand that the free gift of My salvation is not like a transgression. I do not nullify My grace. For if righteousness comes through the law of the works of your hands, My Son would have died, needlessly. And therefore, your faith would be obsolete. But it is because of your faith in Me that righteousness is accounted unto you.

～

Abba Father, thank You for being a God of such remark-able righteousness and grace. You know the errors of our ways, yet credit righteousness unto us when we receive Your righteousness, by way of salvation, into our lives.

I thank You for being so holy and just. You set the standard by which we are to live. Yet, you don't cast us aside for failing to meet that standard. Instead, Your loving grace enables us to be forgiven and to cling to Your righteousness.

Abba Father, You are the perfect example of righteousness. None compares to You. It's an honor to be Your Child and to receive the benefits of Your sacrifice. In Jesus' Name, Amen.

～

Practical Steps:

- Accept that you are justified because of Abba.
- Understand that because of Abba, there is no condemnation.
- Understand that Abba makes you right, not any works of your own.

Father of Sanctification

*And the very God of peace sanctify you wholly; and I pray
God your whole spirit and soul and body be preserved
blameless unto the coming of our Lord Jesus Christ.*

— 1 THESSALONIANS 5:23

I am set apart as a Child of the King!

I speak to the dry places of your life— that they shall be watered, as you hear and receive My words. I decree that a fresh release of breakthrough, miracles, signs, and wonders will show up for you!

Your life shall be that of overflow, as you are set apart for My good use. You shall live a life of sanctification, as I, the Father, have chosen you as first fruits, to be saved through the sanctifying work of the Spirit, and through belief in the truth. As you cleanse yourself from the latter, you will be an instrument for my special purposes— made holy, useful to the Master, and prepared to do any good work.

My child, I long for your oneness with Me. I am your Father and that will never change. I know your earthly parents, caregivers, mentors, or even those that were close to you may have let you down. Their best attempts could never reach you, as I, the Father. I promise, as you open your heart, you will encounter a new measure of faith, a restored union, and conquering love in the Father.

~

Abba Father, thank You for Your love for me. The standard of perfection and purity You set for me will never be met in myself. However, I ask You to examine my inner thoughts and examine my inner heart so that I may identify the areas that need to be rooted out so that the power of Christ might live in me and function through me for Your greater glory.

May you grant me the grace to recognize and root out the impure areas of my life. Allow the Holy Spirit's scalpel of truth to whittle away all that disgraces Your name. Please help me keep my eyes fixed on Jesus Christ, my Lord. Grant me the opportunity to be a vessel fit for your use that has a pure heart and an honest spirit.

I implore you, Lord, search my heart, today. Reveal to me if I have an impure heart, evil intentions, or prideful thoughts. Purify me of everything that is not of You, so that I may be holy and pure in Your sight. In Jesus' Name, Amen.

~

Practical Steps:

- Accept that Abba Father seals His children until redemption.
- Understand that Abba Father stakes ownership over His children.

- Receive God's Word that you are holy, as Abba Father delcares His children, as holy.

Father of Mercy

Let us therefore come boldly unto the throne of grace, that we may obtain mercy, and find grace to help in time of need.

— HEBREWS 4:16

I am merciful to others because of Christ's mercy towards me!

My child, I come to you out of concern. Many days you have cried, pleading for My forgiveness— the weariness of your eyes flushed against the blankets of your pillow. You have spoken in your silence with many tears, wondering if I were even real and where I was. You've even asked the question, "Why did this have to happen if God is real?" My child, I have come to relinquish my touch through the ink of pens to share my heart with you.

You mean so much to me, my child. There's not a moment that I don't think about what concerns you. As your Heavenly Father, I allow you to go through tests to fortify your character and to give you hope.

As a Father who is merciful, I realize many of my children have been blinded by the enemy of fear. My ways are hidden from those who seek me in impatience; the eyes that seek me in human wisdom will never find me. For I am found by those who seek me in simplicity and truth. For my ways are not your ways and my thoughts are not your thoughts. My mercy is given to those who will accept it, yet it's free for all.

As far as the East is from the West, so far hath I removed your transgressions from you. My love for you, My child, is greater than you could ever imagine!

~

Abba Father, thank You for Your great mercy, which springs up every morning and is still steadfast throughout the day. I thank You for the Cross, that's a glorious manifestation of Your love. I was once an outcast and distant from You because of my sin. But because of Your eternal love for me, You sent Your only begotten Son to come to earth as a Man and die on the Cross for my sins. Jesus endured a life of rejection and sorrow. But because of His love for me, He accepted my punishment, endured the process, and gave up His life for me on the Cross of Calvary. And now, I am forgiven of all of my sins and have eternal life with You in heaven.

Abba Father, thank You for showering me with undeserved grace and favor, when I was enslaved in the kingdom of darkness and unworthy to approach Your glorious throne. But because of Your immense mercy and grace, You lifted me out of Satan's bonds. You raised me from the squalid pit of sin, and seated me with Christ in heavenly places.

And in return, Abba, I pray that You use me as a vessel to show others mercy and love without limit. Allow me to

*have the same lovingkindness and forgiveness to others
that You have graciously given to me.*

*Thank You for redeeming me and making me a part of
Your family. In Jesus' Name, Amen.*

~

Practical Steps:

- Receive *Abba Father's* mercy that removed the sting of death that was rightfully ours.
- Understand that Abba Father forgets, but man remembers our shortcomings and failures.
- Accept that Abba Father wants to show you mercy.

Father of Faithfulness

If we believe not, yet he abideth faithful: he cannot deny himself.

— 2 TIMOTHY 2:13

I am covered because of His faithfulness!

My commitment to you has never changed. You are the ardor of My heart. Look not back, but look ahead for My glory is prepared for you. Remain in My love; never face the day without Me. I am your Father and you are My child. I am committed to your care and I will uphold you, build you, and lift you up in your time of need.

As you hold onto My unchanging hand, you will accomplish every task in My strength. I have not taken you out of the world, but I have called you to be a light in the world. The example you set, others will follow. So, lead with grace and allow Me to be your protection and the joy of your strength.

I will turn your bitter tears to sweet perfume. My commitment to you will never fail. I am your faithful Father, riding on the wings of the morning.

As you sleep, I am there. And when you awake, I am near. Never think for one moment that My heart doesn't beat for you. My child, my heart is fused with your heart.

As you abide in Me, I shall abide in you. My child, I shall hide you in the pavilion of My love; my faithfulness towards you will never end.

According to My Word in 2 Timothy 2:13, I am faithful to keep My Word— no matter what— because I cannot deny who I am. I am the way, the truth, and the life (John 14:6). To do anything other than what I say I will do would make Me a liar. And I, Abba Father, am *not* a liar! I am faithful to fulfill every thing I promised (Psalm 71:22). My Word is more dependable than anything you can see or touch!

~

Abba Father, thank You for Your faithfulness through the Cross of Christ, which is a testimony of Your love for me. Your faithful love and compassion provide me with all the things I need in order to live a life designed to please and serve You. Whether knowingly or unknowingly, I humbly repent of the times I rebelled against Your truth. You are so faithful to forgive me, despite how many times I make mistakes.

Abba Father, please revive the grand vision that You designed just for me so that I can be faithful in my service to You. It's my heart to serve You in everything that I do. Your faithfulness towards me is what sustains me. Your amazing faithfulness is the reason that I am still alive.

Abba, please help me to be faithful in my dealings with others, just as You're faithful with me. I want others to come to know by showing Your light in such a dark,

*disgruntled world. Keep me close to You, so that Your
ways become my ways, In Jesus' Name, Amen.*

~

Practical Steps:

- Understand that *Abba Father* is committed to you
- Accept that *Abba Father* is faithful to fulfill every promise
  to you
- Take solace in the loyalty found in *Abba Father's* faithfulness

Father of My Praise

By Him, therefore, let us offer the sacrifice of praise to God continually, that is, the fruit of our lips giving thanks to His Name.

— HEBREWS 13:15

I am honored to praise the King of Kings and Lord of Lords!

What comes to mind when you think about praise? How does it feel to receive praise from someone who tells you how nice you look or how amazing your work is? In contrast, how does it feel when you praise our Heavenly Father? When you consider the natural praise of man to spiritual praise, there's a noticeable contrast between the two.

When children praise their biological fathers, it may bring the fathers joy to hear a heartfelt sound of praise from their children. However, from a spiritual standpoint, our Heavenly Father responds to praise with divine intervention, campaigning upon miracles, signs, and wonders. Praise makes a person respond differently. Sometimes they may even walk better, smell better, and look better, in the natural realm. That's because praise brings about another level of sound in the atmosphere; it shifts, moves, and stirs things up.

We gain a greater sense of joy, peace, happiness, contentment, strength, and other positive emotions when we release praise rather than receive it. We become a better person when we release praise, in contrast to receiving praise about how nice we look or how well we accomplished a task. While the natural responses and feelings for this kind of gratitude from one to another are thoughtful and appreciated, resulting in a good feeling of confidence in one's own abilities, these natural human responses are still no match for the praise we give to our heavenly Father. The reason for this is because when we release praise and adoration, our Heavenly Father pours himself into us and gives us something so much greater, stronger, and more powerful than we can possibly imagine. We are filled with God's divine confidence, wisdom, courage, hope, faith, love, joy, healing, as well as His other attributes— all of which radiate and enhance who we are and who He has made us to be.

There is a two-fold blessing in the release and the pour. Praise attracts the Father; it attracts His attention and causes His glory to abound on earth. Our Heavenly Father inhabits the praises of His people. When we praise, He occupies Himself in our midst. Praising extends an invitation. Through it, the Father can enter. It tells Him that we welcome Him, with open arms. We find answers, deliverance, and healing in our praise. This is why we should never stop praising, even when times are tough. Praise will find you, even when you can't find yourself.

~

Abba Father, thank You for incomparable love for me.
Each moment I spend with you has become more real
to me. When my heart failed You, You kept me.
When I rose against You in utter disregard, You came

after me, realizing that I knew not what I was doing. You made me a nest in the hollow of Your hand, as a father or mother bird protects his or her young. Though the elements raged you gave me peace. And when I was confused, You helped me understand. And for that, I give You praise.

Heavenly Father, You kept me, blowing Your breath of life upon me. There was a time when I felt stuck in the valley of dry bones. But I came alive when You spoke life to me, drenching me with the oil of Your Word until flesh grew upon me and Your spirit restored me. Now, I rise as David, dancing before the King, in honor and admiration of You.

Abba Father, I count it as pure joy to send an upward sound— a breaking sound— in full reverence of You! When You speak, the earth responds to the sound of Your voice. It trembles at Your voice, sending vibrations of joy in the land. I shout before You, knowing that eternity belongs to me. I open up my mouth with unwavering praise, while pursuing territory, as Your hand enlarges my borders.

Abba, Father! I will shout Your Name with a voice of triumph, freely giving all praise to You! Your love has no uncertainty, but assures the one who trusts in You. You are like a bucket of rain pouring out blessings upon me, even in my undeserving state. I am thankful for Your endless love for me; Your love maintains my praise!

∾

Practical Steps:

- Learn to praise *Abba Father* despite the circumstances or how you may feel.
- Understand that *Abba Father* is worthy of all praises.
- Give *Abba Father* the praise that's due His Name!

Father of Life

*He that findeth his life shall lose it: and he that loseth his
life for my sake shall find it.*

— MATTHEW 10:39

I am alive in Christ Jesus!

Have you ever heard a parent say: "I brought you into this
world and I can take you out?" If you ever heard this state-
ment while growing up, your perspective on the value of life
may have shifted. But truth be told, no human has the power to give
or take away life; only God has full power and authority over life.

Sadly, the value of life isn't always respected. There are many who
walk around as if their life belongs to them. Some walk carelessly and
have no consideration for others. Others may live life worrying from day
to day— wondering how they're going to pay their bills, how they're
going to eat, and how to make ends meet, amongst other anxieties. But
when we take a step back and examine the Word, we find that Christ

tells us to take no thought for our lives— what we shall eat or drink. Is not life more than meat and the body more than raiment? Sad to say, many choose to contradict the value God places on life, disregarding its values, morals, integrity, and truths. To some, life appears as a blank canvas to do as one pleases.

When we examine the art sketched paths of life, it can sometimes camouflage the true reality of the triune God, making His existence an understatement. However, the closer we look at life's beautiful art, Christ gives us a clear view that He is the giver and sustainer of all life. It becomes evident that it's only in Him that we move, breathe, and have our being. Every time we are afforded the opportunity to awaken from our sleep and plant our feet upon the floor, we should be reminded of the beautiful gift of life that God has given us.

God has blessed man with the divine gift of creativity. When you walk into a home, you may see floors tiled by the creative ideas of man, surrounded by walls neatly brushed with paint, and cabinets creatively mounted and arranged. Out back, you may view gardens that are neatly clothed with seed-bearing food that is consumed to nourish the human body. From this beautiful display of God's grace, it's easy to see the Hand of God. He has so kindly blessed mankind to enjoy the dainty pleasures of life.

Abba Father gives His children the best, as He delights in seeing His children live life abundantly.

⌁

Abba Father, thank You for giving me life! I am so grateful that Your ways are not like man's ways and that Your thoughts are not like man's thoughts. For You have superseded my limited understanding and expectations of You.

Your love for me is shown in every breath I take, tear I cry, and song I sing. I can truly smile and exude laughter because of Your sincere love for me. I can laugh without fear of the future because You hold life in

Your hands. I never thought in a million years that my life would be drastically changed.

Abba Father, I'm truly grateful; the words I speak cannot express the fullness of my heart towards You. You taught me how to love You as Abba, my Father— a love so real that no one could ever take from me. I'm so overwhelmed by how You love me, looking beyond my faults and seeing my needs.

My need for You drew me towards Your love— the love of a father. Whether man, woman, boy, or girl, You have given the warmness of Your heart as a Father towards all of Your children.

Abba, I thank You for Your mercy and unwavering love that encompasses me. I was lost, but found my way in You. You were always near my side, guiding me along my lonely paths.

Out of the sentiment of my heart flows the treasures of Your love. You have turned my poverty into wealth, my fears into peace, my tears into joy, my hurt into laughter, and my thirst into satisfaction. My anxieties are now under subjection and have no control over me.

Abba Father, Your divine blessings cannot escape me. Father, You have blessed me with good measure that's pressed down, shaken together, and running over. For You, Father, have loved me with an everlasting love, birthing the fullness of life.

$\sim$

Practical Steps:

- Accept *Abba Father's* truth about life.
- Understand that *Abba Father* makes all things new.
- Receive in your soul that Abba Father has given you eternal life in Him.

Father of Strength

(ELOHEI MA'UZZI)

The Lord is my strength and song, and He is become my
salvation: He is my God, and I will prepare Him an
habitation; my father's God, and I will exalt Him.

— EXODUS 15:2

I am strengthened by the power of God!

Imagine a young child dangling from the strong arms of his or her Dad. In this child's eyes, there may be no one stronger than Daddy. This same child may be giggling and playing, as Dad curls his arm to make a big muscle. In the child's mind, he or she may believe that Dad is the strongest person, ever!

When we see innocent, childlike faith displayed through children, it may prompt us to laugh or smile. However, we must remember what Abba Father is saying to us, as well: "Hold my arm. Don't let go. I've got you!" Many times, we may put our faith in the limited abilities of man and think that God has failed us. However, in actuality, we oftentimes fail to stretch our faith and believe Abba Father for limitless possibilities.

Faith is the substance of what we're believing God for. This means that we won't always see it; however, our faith in Abba creates the manifestation of what we're believing Him for. So, as we rely upon the strength and ability of Abba, our faith creates sustainable outcomes that birth the will of God for our life into the earthly realm. This is what causes us to sing:

I will bless the Lord at all times: His praise shall continually be in my mouth. My soul shall make her boast in the Lord: the humble shall hear thereof, and be glad. O magnify the Lord with me, and let us exalt His name together. I sought the Lord, and He heard me, and delivered me from all my fears.

— PSALM 34:1-4

~

Abba Father, thank You for your strength. When the enemy came in like a flood, You lifted up a standard against him. Father, You placed Your spirit upon me and I will not keep silent. I will speak of Your goodness and Your tender mercies. Father, You have renewed my strength so that I might soar on wings like an eagle, run and not grow weary, and walk and not faint.

Abba Father, I have seen Your goodness on my right and on my left. I've beheld Your power; Your glory has not been hidden from me. My eyes swell with tears because my heart is in awe of You. How can one so strong and pure love someone stenched with sin? You have blessed me with the bounties of heaven and have not withheld that which Your heart desires for me.

Abba, You are my place of refuge; when I can't go anywhere else, I know I can trust You. Father, my

weaknesses are upheld by the Blood You've applied to
my life. You washed me and clothed me in Your
Word, leaving no trace of sin, but Your righteousness.

Abba Father, it's because of Your strength that I can
subdue kingdoms and climb mountains.

∽

Practical Steps:

- Accept that *Abba Father* will give you strength in times of weakness.
- Practice leaning upon *Abba Father* for strength.
- Allow *Abba Father* to sustain you when your faith grows weak.

Father of Retribution

When He maketh inquisition for blood, He remembereth them: He forgetteth not the cry of the humble.

— PSALM 9:12

I am defended by the King!

Our Father of retribution comes to our defense. He said that when our enemies come in like a flood, the Spirit of the Lord will lift up a standard against our enemies and put them to flight. Abba, Father fights for us, never leaving us alone. When a thousand fall on our left and ten thousand on our right, Abba forbids it to come near us.

As a child, it's easy to remember all the times Abba Father came to our rescue. His Word declares that no weapon formed against us can prosper. And He has always been in our corner, no matter what. There were even moments when He stood back to see we would behave. And even when He was silent during those times, He has never left our side.

As we got older, Abba trained our hands to war, teaching us how to fight spiritual battles. For the weapons of our warfare are not carnal, but mighty through Abba Father to pull down of every stronghold!

No battle can be won without Abba! We attain victory only through the power of righteousness and the Holy Spirit. Abba, will advocate for us and punish our enemies. Abba Father is our fortress, high tower, deliverer, and shield— we can trust in Him. He subdued our enemies under our feet. The punishment rendered to our enemies outweighs the price we could have paid. Abba Father truly fights for us!

❧

Abba Father, thank You for Your love that compelled You allow Your Son to bear the weight of sin for me. Therefore, Abba, I can serve no one, but You! Father, I put away my idols and give You my heart.

Abba Father, You paid it all. With the shedding of Your Blood, You washed away my sins, allowing my soul to drink from the rivers of water. Father, I lay my heart before You, leaving none of me— only desiring all of You.

Father, I take upon me the helmet of salvation, the breastplate of righteousness, truth girded around my loins, the preparation of the gospel of peace on my feet, the shield of faith, and the sword of the spirit.

Jesus Christ committed no sin; no deceit was found in His mouth. He bore my sins in His body on the Cross so that I might die to sin and live for righteousness. And by His wounds, I am healed. The retribution of Your Son's love for me caused Him to take the punishment for my sins. It was His life that gave me life, and I'm grateful for it. The price that was paid, gave me the freedom to live because Jesus Christ already paid it all.

❧

Practical Steps:

- Accept that *Abba Father* has vindicated our souls.
- Understand that *Abba Father* helps when things are seemingly impossible and appear as though there is no hope
- Receive the peace that *Abba Father* brings.

Father of Help

I am supported by my Father!

When we're faced with test at school, work, or in life in general, Abba Father helps us get through. When you think of the movie *The Help*, you may recall that assistance was requested. Likewise, many people can hire maids to help them keep their home furnishings in excellent condition. But in our earthen vessels, Abba Father gives us His Word to help us through the tests and trials of this world.

Sometimes in life, we may find ourselves in positions of needing help or additional assistance. And for some individuals, it may be challenging to ask for help due to their negative experiences with others.

Many have indicated that they don't like to ask for help because they don't want it to be thrown in their face later or have those same individuals bragging about what they've done for them. Other times, it's simply an issue of pride that prohibits the individual from asking for help. There are many levels to this!

When we consider the concept of help, we may think of an individual in need of assistance or someone who has an emergency that involves the welfare of a child. For some, providing them with support can be embarrassing, offensive, or even painful. But despite all of this, Abba Father knows and understands the frailties and human weakness of man.

Abba Father understands that we need more than just surface-level help. Therefore, He offered Himself as a sacrifice to help others who would not be able to overcome on their own without Him. Abba has never made a mockery of His children. He gently helps us, loves us, and calls us to wholeness, without bringing shame to us regarding our need for Him. There is never a time that our Heavenly Father makes us feel less than His own.

In Romans 8 :1, Abba Father reminds us that, "There is now no condemnation for those who are in Christ Jesus." Therefore, when you and I walk around in condemnation and defeat, it makes an understatement of our Father's ability to do and be who He says He is in our lives.

Abba, promised to help you. You are His child; there is nothing He will not do for you. Whether you're taking an exam, desire salvation, have an addiction, need healing, struggling in a marriage, or facing challenging moments with your children, He wants to help you! Therefore, when you find yourself being in a moment where you need help, reach out to Abba. He will either send you the help you need, or adjust the circumstances and make a way of escape for you. Regardless of either option, He will ensure that you receive His help and support.

Abba Father, thank You for all of Your support. When I

fell down, You helped me. You directed my steps, while delighting in every detail of my life. Though I stumbled, You never allowed me to fall and stay there.

Abba Father, Your love has guided me all my days. In my youthful years, You held me in Your hands, as one would assist a child who is riding a bike for the first time— susceptible to many falls. You embraced me like a child who first learns how to run, falling repetitively, but getting back up stronger each time. You held my hand until I was able to sustain balance. But no matter what, You always remained close, just in case I fell again. And in those moments, You've caught me every time and ensured that I was properly cared for.

Abba Father, I can't survive without Your divine help. Thank You for showing me what true love is!

∾

Practical Steps:

- Understand that *Abba Father* has your best interest at heart.
- Accept the wisdom that *Abba Father* provides.
- Allow *Abba Father* to help you.

Father of Sight

And she called the name of the Lord that spake unto her,
Thou God seest me.

— GENESIS 16:13A

I am regarded by my loving Father in Heaven!

I will give you sight to see. When you don't know which way to go, I will give you dreams and visions that will show you what's to come. I will not deny My presence from you; you have seen Me in many facets of your life. None can compare to the love relationship I have with you. The moments you seek me, searching for My hand in love, I hold you as a Father would, protecting you from the tempest and raging storms.

My child, you mean so much to Me. Many words cannot articulate the divine union we have. You are anointed to discern time— days, years, and seasons. As I give instruction, take heed to follow the path I lay before you. Though waters may rise, I will make your path straight and settle the storms. You will not be without opposition, but you must remember that My spirit has already gone out before you. I will not leave you in this alone.

Write the vision and make it plain upon tables, so that those who read it may carry it out. I will show you things to come— as My Word has spoken— things beyond human comprehension. Although you won't become familiar or always be able to understand the great kindness that I will show you, continue to rest in My promises.

I, the Lord your Father, gives sight to the blind and feet to the lame. If I lifted up those who were bowed down, what will I not do for My own children that have come into My kingdom? I love righteousness. There are no limits to the wisdom and vision that I will give to you; you have proven your love to Me.

My child, you have carried your cross, even amidst difficult situations. You did not give up, even when many voices told you to throw in the towel. My child, you stood your ground, declaring that your Heavenly Father lives. I know you may not always understand the things I show you, but stay at My feet. I will continue to give you insight into new realms and sharpen your ears to hear what the Father is dispersing to you.

My child, you're very peculiar. You have tapped into places where many cannot go. Your love for Me is so pure that you often feel misunderstood because many have not gone where you have in My presence. There are only a few that can go where you have gone. Our fellowship is pure devotion; don't limit yourself because people don't understand. Never compromise the anointing I placed upon your life because of the frail thinking of man. You are my chosen one. You are very special to me and nothing will ever change that, My child.

I am Abba Father. I see all and know all things. I see your plans and desires for your life. But trust that I hold the future and your destiny in My hands.

~

Abba Father, thank You for seeing and knowing what's best for me. Your Word says that You know the plans You have for me, that of good and not of evil. You see

*my beginning and the end; it was Your hands that
formed me and blew the breath of life into my mortal
body. Your life gave me life. Your love taught me how
to love. And for that, I can't praise You enough.*

*Abba Father, You've made so many ways for me. Likewise,
you've opened and closed many doors because you
foreknew my destiny. Your plans for me were already
preordained since the beginning of time.*

*Your Word says that we should live by faith and not by
sight. Father, a thousand years in your sight are like a
day that has just gone by.*

*Abba Father, I pray that Your love and faithfulness never
leave me. Help me to bind them around my neck and
write them on the tablet of my heart so that I will win
favor and have a good name in the sight of You
and man.*

~

Practical Steps:

- Allow *Abba Father* to open your eyes to what He sees is best for your present and future.
- Receive the guidance *Abba Father* provides.
- Adjust your perspective as *Abba Father* exposes you to deeper truth and revelation.

Father of Dependability

Heaven and earth shall pass away: but my words shall not pass away.

— MARK 13:31

I am secure because the Word of God is everlasting!

S ometimes, as a people, we can become so independent from God. We may choose to depend on our parents, jobs, side hustles, children, and many other things to uphold us. Despite our ignorance, God desires to teach us how to depend on Him— alone. But sometimes, we may opt to depend on the church instead of establishing our own intimate relationship with Abba Father. It is essential that we learn to communicate regularly with Him and rely solely on His strength.

For many of us, depending on others to meet a need isn't something we particularly enjoy. We understand what it's like to express a heartfelt desire, but may not be comfortable with the feeling of needing help.

On occasion, you may walk down a street and hear individuals ramping and raging, screaming, "I don't need you!" Their adrenaline may be non-stop, as they parade their frustrations abruptly to one another. This may sound like two individuals who have so much pride, that they've allowed the issues of life to stir their emotions in unhealthy ways. They may say things such as, "I don't need you," "Forget you," "I don't care," or "I can do it all on my own!"

There may be mothers who have separated a child from the father, out of anger, trying to prove a point of independence and highlight his parenting irrelevance. Or, there may be fathers who have held back love and attention from a child who so desperately needs them because of how they feel towards the mother.

There are widespread scenarios surrounding the topic of dependability. However, it's important to understand how our Heavenly Father relates to this. Our Heavenly Father's desire is for us to rely and depend solely on Him, because he knows we cannot make it without Him. Although our human nature wants us to believe that we can survive life's trauma's, obstacles, and whirlwinds of life all on our own, we know deep within that we cannot make this life without God. We may have someone in our corner who will care, undergird, and support us in our weakest, most vulnerable moments in life— however, we cannot make it without depending on God.

We must understand that our Heavenly Father is the oxygen to every situation. He keeps us alive and breathing. Therefore, it's easy to recall several situations in our lives where we can assuredly say that if it had not been for the mercy and grace of God, we don't know where we would be.

Abba Father seeks our very existence; He desires us to cling to the garments of His love. And at no time will He ever reject or turn away from your need for Him. He instructs us to trust in Him and lean not to our own understanding. Rather, in all our ways we must acknowledge him and He will direct our path.

Our dependence on Abba does not come with human conditions. He does not make you feel less than, ashamed, impotent, or any other debased feeling because of your need for Him. Abba understands that His children are forever learning and coming into the full knowledge and wisdom of who He is. It's His desire to lead us along paths of righteousness so that we may be full of Him, resemble our Father, and take on new life in Christ with exceeding joy.

~

Abba Father, thank You for being my Rock. For so long, I've trusted in my strength and the strength of mere humans to guide me down paths only You could. I've trusted in the wealth of the land through jobs and other means of income and support, without trusting you. Father, I even trusted in frail relationships to fill voids that only You could fill. But yet, you've never given up on me.

Abba Father, when I came to you like the prodigal son, You never turned Your back on me. Instead, You held me, kissed me, and loved me like no one ever could. I relented into Your arms, thrusting my heart against Yours. It was a warmness I never wanted to let go of. Although You forgave me, I somehow found it hard to believe that someone could love me this much beyond my weaknesses, limitations, and frailties.

Father, I am consumed by Your love and draped in Your mercy. You took hold of my right hand, leading me along paths that I never thought I'd walk, touching me in places no mere human has ever been.

Father, I long for Your companionship. I thirst for Your love. Your strength has secured me and Your compassion has held me. Father, I trust You with all of my heart. I no longer lean on my own understanding. I submit all of my ways to You so that You will make my paths straight. Thank you, Abba Father for being so dependable and establishing my steps. In Jesus' Name, Amen.

~

Practical Steps:

- Identify the ways that *Abba Father* has been dependable in your life.
- Receive the guidance and correction that *Abba Father* desires to give you.
- Celebrate *Abba Father's* dependable love for you that sustains, maintains, and keeps you throughout all of life's challenges.

Father of My Exceeding Joy

Then will I go unto the altar of God, unto God my
exceeding joy: yea, upon the harp will I praise thee, O
God my God.

— PSALM 43:4

I am joyful in the presence of God!

Now that I have come to know who I am as a child of the true and living God, I can rejoice with exceeding gladness, knowing that I am not on this journey alone. I understand that my joy is in Abba Father, and Him alone. Abba makes all things well. I shall go out in joy and be led forth in peace. The mountains and the hills before me shall break forth into singing, along with the trees of the field.

When we search the world for happiness and empty pleasures to fulfill the places only Abba Father can fill, we find ourselves in repetitious cycles of vanities. The Word of God in Ecclesiastes 1 puts it this way: "What profit hath a man of all his labour which he taketh under the sun? One generation passeth away, and another generation cometh: but the earth abideth for ever" (Ecclesiastes 1:3-4). Later in the chapter, it states, "I have seen all the works that are done under the sun; and behold , all is vanity and vexation of spirit" (Ecclesiastes 1:14).

In this passage, Scripture informs us that the pleasures of life are just temporary gain. However, in contrast, the exceeding joy of Abba Father is forever, even unto eternity. The Word of God states, "There's no greater joy than to hear my children walk in truth" (3 John 1:4). He is Abba, your Father, and in Him you will find exceeding great joy.

～

Abba Father, thank You for being my help. In the shadow of Your wings, I will sing for joy. My soul clings to You. Your right hand upholds me, causing my soul to rejoice, always. I shall give thanks in every situation and circumstance, for this is Your will for me, in Christ Jesus.

In you Father, I shall go out in joy and be led forth in peace; the mountains and the hills before me shall break forth into singing. All the trees of the field shall sing Your name! You have made known to me the paths of life; You will make me full of gladness with Your presence. And my spirit rejoices in God, my Savior.

Abba Father, You have no greater joy than to hear that Your children are walking in truth. Father, I delight in Your truth; Your Word is truth! Hallelujah! Your Word is food to my soul; it's the joy and delight of my heart. For I am called by Your name, o Lord, God of hosts. I will forever experience true joy in You. In Jesus' Name, Amen.

～

Practical Steps:

- Bask in the unending joy of *Abba Father*.
- Be a carrier of *Abba Father's* joy unto others.
- Be transformed by the joy of *Abba Father*.

Son of God

For God so loved the world, that He gave His only begotten
Son, that whosoever believeth in Him should not
perish, but have everlasting life.

— JOHN 3:16

I am loved by the One who shed His Blood for me!

Many people did not believe Jesus was the Son of God. He was in front of them, but they didn't recognize Him as the light. Many mocked Jesus, casting lots over His garments; they looked at Him as a weak, mortal man, not realizing the power He held in just His Name alone— Jesus! Humbly, He entered this world without making a name for Himself. And in exchange for your life, He gave His.

Jesus, as the only begotten Son of God, suffered, bled, and died so that you might be redeemed and resurrected to eternal life. As such, if you remain in Him, He is faithful to remain in you, cleansing you of your ways and filling you with more of Himself.

Although God exists as three persons, He operates in harmony with Himself— as one. His very essence, nature, power, action, and will are equal and co-eternal. The confines of words have no placement of Him. The finite mindset of man cannot contain Him.

He is God in all of His divinity - Father, Son, and Holy Spirit. Among us dwells the one and only, living God. It was announced before Jesus was born that He would be called the Son of God.

Jesus Christ– Son of God– is the way, the truth, and the life! No one comes to the Father except through Him. You must believe, by faith, that Jesus Christ has overcome the world and has brought you life! As a result, when you accept the Son of God as Lord of your life, you now have eternal life.

The will of God is that none should perish. Thus, being obedient to God's will is crucial. Trust His guidance and instruction. Surrender all of your ways, desires, rebellion, and disobedience. Let His salvation envelop you. He has prepared a path for you that is filled with peace, joy, love, hope, prosperity, kindness, abundance, and laughter. God wants to bless you, abundantly. Welcome Him into your life, today.

～

Abba Father, thank You for sending Your only begotten Son, Jesus Christ, to die on the Cross for my sins. Without His shed Blood, there would be no life for me. I don't take for granted the peace that comes with knowing that I am eternally redeemed and have new, everlasting life in You.

Because of Jesus Christ— the Son of God— I can now have access to You, Abba Father. In Your Word, You said that through Your Son, I can now have access to You. The veil was torn and now I can come boldly before Your throne of grace.

Thank you, Abba Father, for loving me so much. You made a way for me to have life. For that, I am truly grateful. Your lovingkindness is matchless. Your long-suffering and peace are irreplaceable. I am eternally thankful for Your sacrifice. In Jesus' Name, Amen.

~

Practical Steps:

- Open your heart to receive love from the *Son of God*.
- Understand that the *Son of God* has come to redeem you back to Abba Father.
- Accept Jesus Christ as the *Son of God*.

Child of God

But as many as received Him, to them gave He power to become the sons of God, even to them that believe on His Name.

— JOHN 1:12

I am a Child of God through my faith in Him.

As a citizen, we have rights, as well as regulations. Within society, we are granted certain liberties, but also required to function according to the laws that govern us. When we comply with such directives, we operate in obedience to the government, and are considered law-abiding citizens.

From a natural standpoint, these directives stand true and are commonly accepted. But what about God's kingdom? Have you ever considered what our position as a Child of God grants us?

In order to know your rights, you must first understand *who* you are. And in order to exercise your rights, you must first know *what* they are! These truths will affect the way you live.

When you accept Jesus Christ as your personal Lord and Savior, you become a citizen of His Kingdom and His Child. As His Child, you are entitled to many benefits, which include:

- Freedom (John 8:36)
- Healing (Isaiah 53:5)
- Prosperity (2 Corinthians 9:8)
- Peace (Psalm 29:11)
- Power (1 John 3:23)
- Victory (2 Corinthians 2:14)

Ultimately, knowing your position defines your self-image. You will see yourself differently and based upon how Heaven sees you! You will no longer accept what's not yours or settle for less than what you're worth. After all, you are a *Child of the King*!

My Child, you belong to Me. But as many as received Me, to them I gave power to become My sons and daughters, even to those that believe on My Name.

~

Abba Father, thank You for adopting me and accepting me into Your family. It's an honor to be Yours. I now carry your DNA and spiritual makeup. The Blood of Jesus is what establishes me into Your family. It regenerates me and gives me a new identity.

Being a Child of God grants me the privilege of protection, as I am covered and safe against all outside attacks. There is safety in being Yours. And for that, I am so thankful.

As Your Child, it's a blessing to receive Your continual love and grace. There are many promises that accompany the blessing of being Yours. I pray that I never lose

sight of the blessing of having a relationship with You.
In Jesus' Name, Amen.

~

Practical Steps:

- Accept your new identity in Jesus Christ as a *Child of God*.
- Refuse to settle because a *Child of God* is royalty.
- Adjust your thought pattern to reflect His truth about you as a *Child of God*.
- Behave according to your worth as a *Child of God*.

Acknowledgments

*This book would not be possible without the
love and support of my family:*

Thank you to my children— Devontae, Da'montae, Emmanuel, and Colin— your unending love has inspired me to stay focused and never give up! The lessons I've learned through parenting taught me the virtues of love. I'm truly grateful for each moment God has given me to parent and to be parented by Him.

Thank you to my mom— Gloria— who stood on the foundation of prayer and God's Word. You taught my siblings and I the purity of God's love through his Word. This is how I found my way back to God when all seemed lost.

About the Author

Tiffany McCullough, a native of Baltimore, Maryland, is a mother, author, minister, Christian Counselor, Licensed Childcare Professional, and Family and Youth Activist. But most importantly, she is a lover of Christ who has dedicated her life to serving families, internationally, through the revelation of God's love. As CEO of A New Revelation World Outreach, her mission is to rebuild the family infrastructure by providing developmental resources geared toward wholeness and restoration. Tiffany stands firmly on the Word of God— all things are possible, no matter how things may appear! She firmly believes that every family can thrive, living a healthy, wholesome life— physically, spiritually, psychologically, and socially.

Made in the USA
Middletown, DE
09 March 2023

26380789R00071